Endorsements for the Church Questions Series

"Christians are pressed by very real questions. How does Scripture structure a church, order worship, organize ministry, and define biblical leadership? Those are just examples of the questions that are answered clearly, carefully, and winsomely in this new series from 9Marks. I am so thankful for this ministry and for its incredibly healthy and hopeful influence in so many faithful churches. I eagerly commend this series."

R. Albert Mohler Jr., President, The Southern Baptist Theological Seminary

"Sincere questions deserve thoughtful answers. If you're not sure where to start in answering these questions, let this series serve as a diving board into the pool. These minibooks are winsomely to-the-point and great to read together with one friend or one hundred friends."

Gloria Furman, author, *Missional Motherhood* and *The Pastor's Wife*

"As a pastor, I get asked lots of questions. I'm approached by unbelievers seeking to understand the gospel, new believers unsure about next steps, and maturing believers wanting help answering questions from their Christian family, friends, neighbors, or coworkers. It's in these moments that I wish I had a book to give them that was brief, answered their questions, and pointed them in the right direction for further study. Church Questions is a series that provides just that. Each booklet tackles one question in a biblical, brief, and practical manner. The series may be called Church Questions, but it could be called 'Church Answers.' I intend to pick these up by the dozens and give them away regularly. You should too."

Juan R. Sanchez, Senior Pastor, High Pointe Baptist Church, Austin, Texas

Is It Loving to Practice Church Discipline?

Church Questions

Is It Loving to Practice Church Discipline?

Jonathan Leeman

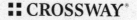
CROSSWAY®

WHEATON, ILLINOIS

Trade paperback ISBN: 978-1-4335-7025-4
ePub ISBN: 978-1-4335-7028-5
PDF ISBN: 978-1-4335-7025-4
Mobipocket ISBN: 978-1-4335-7027-8

Library of Congress Cataloging-in-Publication Data

Names: Leeman, Jonathan, 1973- author.
Title: Is it loving to practice church discipline? / Jonathan Leeman.
Description: Wheaton, Illinois : Crossway, [2020] | Series: Church questions | Includes bibliographical references and index.
Identifiers: LCCN 2020003074 (print) | LCCN 2020003075 (ebook) | ISBN 9781433570254 (trade paperback) | ISBN 9781433570254 (pdf) | ISBN 9781433570278 (mobi) | ISBN 9781433570285 (epub)
Subjects: LCSH: Church discipline. | Church discipline—Biblical teaching.
Classification: LCC BV740 .L445 2020 (print) | LCC BV740 (ebook) | DDC 262/.8—dc23
LC record available at https://lccn.loc.gov/2020003074
LC ebook record available at https://lccn.loc.gov/2020003075

Crossway is a publishing ministry of Good News Publishers.

BP			29	28	27	26	25	24	23	22	21	20
15	14	13	12	11	10	9	8	7	6	5	4	3	2	1

No discipline seems pleasant at the time, but painful. Later on, however, it produces a harvest of righteousness and peace for those who have been trained by it.

Hebrews 12:11 NIV

Do you remember the first time you heard the phrase "church discipline"? Perhaps it felt a little jarring. You didn't expect those two words to go together, just like you don't expect the pairing of "painful friendship" or "conditional grace."

After all, churches should represent love and mercy, not judgment or discipline. Right?

How much stranger, then, would it sound for me to suggest that church discipline is actually loving. Would that throw you for a loop?

Yet that's what this booklet will suggest. I want to show you what church discipline is and how it works. But more than that, I want to help you see that it *is* loving and that it even shows us something about the love of God. Still sound strange? Perhaps we need a better understanding of church discipline—and a better understanding of love.

Church Discipline Is Not Always Loving

To be sure, church discipline is not always loving. Maybe, like me, you read Nathaniel Hawthorne's *The Scarlet Letter* in high school. Set in seventeenth-century New England, the novel tells the fictional story of a strong and beautiful woman who becomes pregnant out of wedlock. She never gives up the father's name, which only enflames the town where church and state are blended to the point of being nearly the same entity.

The governing authorities discipline her first by requiring her to wear an embroidered scarlet letter "A" on her dress. The "A" stands for adulteress. Then they require her to live outside the town in a wilderness cabin, like an "unclean"

Israelite excluded from the camp in the Old Testament.

Meanwhile, we (the readers) learn that her partner in crime, the newborn's father, is the town pastor. The only thing worse than the town and church's judgment is the pastor's hypocrisy in letting the unwed mother take the fall alone. Love in this book, it turns out, shows itself only in the ostracized woman and the young daughter she raises.

To contemporary ears, Hawthorne's story of church discipline, with its soap-opera storyline, can feel a bit cartoonish. Yet we also need to face the reality that churches are not always loving or wise in practicing church discipline. Sometimes churches bind consciences where Scripture does not bind them. Sometimes they blame the wrong parties. And sometimes they even show favor to the leaders and prejudice toward the hurting member.

We need to acknowledge the difference between loving church discipline and unloving church discipline. Abusive church discipline, like abusive parents or police officers, does great damage. It's hateful, and God hates it.

Church Discipline Grows a Church in Righteousness and Peace

But we cannot throw the baby out with the bathwater, like throwing out the whole idea of marriage because you witness a bad one. Jesus himself gave us church discipline, as we'll see in a bit. Loving church discipline yields life, health, holiness, and growth. It helps our churches stay healthy and furthers the witness of the gospel.

Scripture teaches that discipline and love are actually closely connected: "The Lord disciplines the one he loves" (Heb. 12:6). God doesn't regard love and discipline as being at odds but teaches that love motivates discipline. The author of Hebrews continues, "God disciplines us for our good, in order that we may share in his holiness. No discipline seems pleasant at the time, but painful. Later on, however, it produces a harvest of righteousness and peace for those who have been trained by it" (vv. 10–11

NIV). That phrase "harvest of righteousness and peace" makes me think of golden fields of wheat, only I imagine that those fields are righteousness and peace in a church. Doesn't that sound like a beautiful picture?

In the same way that correcting a student's math mistakes grows the student, so loving discipline grows the church. It grows the individual involved as well as everyone who participates.

I remember one trusted sister in Christ saying to me in a straightforward manner, "Jonathan, you can be really selfish." That little informal act of discipline helped me. I honestly didn't realize I was as selfish as she said I was. She helped me to see my error and grow.

I remember another occasion when our elders stood before our church and informed us that a member had left his wife and children. They were asking for our help in calling the man back from his sin and informing us of the possibility of removing him from the church. A couple nights later I had dinner with David, a younger man in the church. Before dropping him off at his house, he turned to me and said,

Is Discipline Really Biblical?

Yet before we go any further, the most important question we should ask is, *Is church discipline really in the Bible?*

The answer is, yes, it shows up in a number of New Testament passages (for instance, see 2 Cor. 2:6; Gal. 6:1; Eph. 5:11; 1 Thess. 5:14; 2 Thess. 3:6–15; 1 Tim. 5:19–20; 2 Tim. 3:2–5; Titus 3:10). Perhaps the two most well-known passages on church discipline are Matthew 18:15–17 and 1 Corinthians 5.

Matthew 18

Jesus raises the topic in Matthew 18 while teaching about how a good shepherd will leave the ninety-nine sheep to pursue the one stray (vv. 10–14). How do we pursue the one stray? Jesus answers like this:

> If your brother sins against you, go and tell him his fault, between you and him alone. If he listens to you, you have gained your brother. But if he does not listen, take one or

two others along with you, that every charge
may be established by the evidence of two
or three witnesses. If he refuses to listen to
them, tell it to the church. And if he refuses
to listen even to the church, let him be to you
as a Gentile and a tax collector. (vv. 15–17)

So someone is sinning. He's confronted privately. He doesn't stop. He's confronted a second
time. He still doesn't stop. He's confronted by the
church. He still doesn't stop. At that point, Jesus
says, he should be treated as someone outside the
covenant community—as an outsider. He must be
excluded or excommunicated from the fellowship.

Notice Jesus wants to keep the matter as small
as possible, but he's also willing to take a matter to
the whole church. After all, it's the whole church
that affirmed that person's profession of faith when
they brought him into membership. In a church,
we all share in that mutual affirmation because we
share a family name. We are responsible for one
another, like different parts of the body.

Notice also that Jesus believes in due process.
A matter must be established by two or three

witnesses, just like in a Jewish court of law (Deut. 19:15). He doesn't want false charges or mob justice to rule the church. He doesn't want pastors standing up and offering their interpretations of people's character. He only wants churches to act when the facts are generally agreed upon.

Still, Jesus's words might seem startling. Didn't he just tell us a few chapters earlier, "Judge not, that you be not judged" (Matt. 7:1)? The interesting thing is, Jesus told his disciples not to judge in the same breath that he told them not to cast their pearls before pigs and to recognize a tree by its fruits, both of which involve judgment (7:6, 20). How do we put all this together? Apparently, Jesus does *not* want us to presume to act as someone's final judge, but he *does* want us to exercise discernment in whom we fellowship with, particularly when it comes to membership in a church.

1 Corinthians 5

Paul teaches the same thing in 1 Corinthians 5. He confronts the Corinthian church about a member who is sleeping with his father's wife (v. 1). The church already knows about the situation, but for some reason they are proud. Perhaps they think they are being loving and tolerant? Whatever the case may be, Paul replies that they should not be proud but instead should "let him who has done this be removed from among you" (v. 2).

Notice that Paul's process looks a little different than Jesus's. Jesus offered a four-step process: first the one, then the two or three, then the church, then the removal. Yet Paul tells the church to remove the man immediately. Why the difference between Jesus and Paul? Two reasons stand out. First, Jesus's process moves step by step in order to test a person's repentance, whereas Paul has already determined that this man is unrepentant (vv. 3, 11). Second, Jesus presents a scenario where the offense is private and unknown, whereas Paul tells us the whole Corinthian church already knows. In other words, Paul's real situation begins where Jesus's example situation ends.

What's the takeaway? There is no one-size-fits-all process for church discipline. Each one needs to be handled carefully and wisely, attending to the particular facts of the case and any relevant background details. Is this person a brand-new Christian or an old Christian? A well-taught member or a recent member? A rebellious person or a weak person? Was she caught or did she initiate confession? Does he fully own his sin or just a part of it? Is she willing to inconvenience herself as part of her repentance, or does she insist on doing everything her own way? Does he follow through on his promises or not? Do any words of apology sound like godly sorrow or worldly sorrow (2 Cor. 7:10)? What role did others play? Was she led astray?

Each case requires extraordinary pastoral care, caution, wisdom, and love. We might even say, it's not enough for a church to be loving. It must also be wise. And it's not enough for a church to be wise. It must also be loving.

First Corinthians 5 also helps us to see the purpose of discipline. First, *discipline exposes*.

Sin, like cancer, loves to hide. Discipline exposes the cancer of sin so that it might be cut out (see v. 2).

Second, *discipline warns*. A church does not enact God's judgment through discipline. Rather, it stages a small play that pictures the great judgment to come (v. 5).

Third, *discipline saves*. Churches pursue it when they see a member taking the path toward death and none of their arm-waving causes him or her to stop. It's the church's last resort (v. 5).

Fourth, *discipline protects*. Just as cancer spreads from one cell to another, so sin quickly spreads from one person to another (v. 6).

Fifth, *discipline preserves the church's witness*. As strange as it may sound, discipline serves non-Christians because it keeps churches distinct and attractive (see v. 1). After all, churches are to be salt and light. "But if salt has lost its taste," Jesus said, "it is no longer good for anything except to be thrown out and trampled under people's feet" (Matt. 5:13).[1]

What Is Church Discipline?

I think we've seen plenty of evidence that church discipline is in the Bible. But we still haven't answered the question, What is church discipline?

Teach and Correct

You might have noticed that "disciple" and "discipline" are related words. In the broadest sense, church discipline is one part of Christian discipleship.[2] It involves teaching *and* correction. Not surprisingly, there's a centuries-old practice of referring to "formative discipline" and "corrective discipline." We form by teaching. We correct by pointing out error.

Discipline, then, is like any number of things involving teaching and correction, such as teaching math or being a doctor. Both involve teaching and correcting. What would you think of a math teacher who explains the lesson but never corrects her students' mistakes? Or a doctor who talks about health but ignores cancer?

In the same way, making Christian disciples involves teaching and correcting. It's comparatively easy to talk about the teaching side. It's a little harder to talk about the correcting side. I don't like to be corrected, do you? But making disciples without correcting sin makes as much sense as a doctor who ignores tumors.

More narrowly, church discipline means *correcting sin*. The process begins with private warnings. It ends, when necessary, with removing someone from church membership and participation in the Lord's Table for unrepentant sin—sin they refuse to let go of. Often, people use the words "church discipline" to refer especially to this last step, as when they say, "We disciplined Joe from the church," meaning they removed Joe from membership in the church and the Table. They might also use the word "excommunication" (think ex-communion) to mean the same thing.

Someone who has been disciplined out of a church or excommunicated should generally remain free to attend the church's public gatherings, but he or she is no longer a member. He or she should no longer take the Lord's Supper.

And the church will no longer publicly affirm the person's profession of faith.

Church discipline is not about retribution or enacting justice. It's redemptive. It's meant to help the individual Christian and the congregation grow in godliness—in God-like-ness. As Paul says, "deliver this man to Satan for the destruction of the flesh, so that his spirit may be saved" (1 Cor. 5:5).

Yes, the final step of church discipline—excommunication—offers a small picture of judgment in the present (see 1 Cor. 5:12), but that picture lovingly warns of an even greater judgment to come (e.g., 1 Cor. 5:5). How merciful of God to warn his people of the great judgment to come in comparatively small ways now!

What Exactly Does Removing Someone from a Church Say about the Person?

When a church removes someone from membership, what exactly are they declaring by doing this? Does it mean the church is sending someone to hell? No, that is an older Roman Catholic teaching.

Does it mean that a church is declaring with absolute certainty that someone is a non-Christian? Again, no, Jesus did not give the church a God's-eye-view into someone's heart.

Rather, removing a person from membership and participation in the Lord's Supper is a way of declaring that a church is no longer willing to affirm publicly that someone is a Christian.

Think for a second about what a church is saying when it brings a person into membership. The church is publicly affirming an individual's profession of faith. It is declaring before the nations, "Joe professes to be a follower of Christ, and we hereby publicly testify that we agree with him. We believe Joe is a citizen of Christ's kingdom." The church makes this declaration through baptism and the Lord's Supper.

So if membership involves the church's public affirmation of a profession, church discipline involves the removal of that affirmation. The person may continue to profess he or she is a Christian. Yet now the church says, "We can no longer affirm this."

Or let me explain it this way. If "Joe" came up to you and told you he was *not* a Christian, and then I asked you whether Joe was a Christian, you would say, "No." Right?

But suppose Joe said he was a Christian, yet then you watched him do something we don't expect of Christians and not apologize for it, like leaving his wife for another woman. What would you say if I asked you whether he was a Christian then? I expect you would probably feel uncomfortable offering an absolute "yes" or "no." Removing someone from membership in the church, likewise, is not an absolute "yes" or "no" in response to someone's profession of faith. It is the removal of the "yes." It is saying "we will no longer affirm this profession." A church reaches a point where, after multiple attempts to call a person to repentance, it feels dishonest continuing to affirm a person's profession of faith.

For instance, when my church removed "Sam," a single man, for unrepentant sexual sin, he was still calling himself a Christian. But he was refusing to stop his sinful sexual activity. He had a choice between Jesus and his sin, and he wanted to insist he could keep both—suggesting he loved his sin more than Jesus. Therefore, after several months, multiple conversations, and much prayer, the church voted to remove Sam. We could no longer affirm his profession.

Two implications follow from all of this. First, when a person stops calling themselves a Christian, I don't believe a church should excommunicate that person. Instead it should let the person resign. There is no public record to correct. The person has corrected it him or herself. This is why Paul says a church should withhold the hand of fellowship to "anyone who bears the name of brother" and yet is living in unrepentant sin (1 Cor. 5:11).

Second, church discipline is the breaking of Christian fellowship or a church relationship. It is not the breaking of a family relationship. Wives of excommunicated husbands should still fulfill all the biblical duties of a wife to a husband. Sons of excommunicated mothers should still honor and care for their mothers.

Is Church Discipline Really Loving?

If church discipline is a relatively new topic to you, you probably still have a number of practical questions, such as "Which sins lead to discipline?" or "How does all this work?" I will address some of these questions in a few moments because they are crucial for rounding out exactly what church discipline is. But before I do, let's tackle our main question head on: Is church discipline really loving?

The short answer is, it depends on which universe you live in.

Getting Love All Wrong

If you live in a universe in which humanity is at the center, and we human beings are the measure of all things, then, no, church discipline is not loving. Love in this human-centric universe is about helping people to discover themselves, define themselves, create themselves, express themselves. Love in this universe doesn't put moral constraints on people other than not hurting others because others are the centers of their own universes too. Such love claims to never correct, never judge, never impose an "objective" truth. The only truth it insists upon is being true to oneself.

My daughters learned this kind of love watching Disney princess movies. Ariel in *The Little Mermaid* wanted to love whom she loved, not whom her father wanted her to love. Belle in *Beauty and the Beast* wanted to write her own life story, not the life story her little village would have imposed on her. And, of course, Elsa in *Frozen* boldly sang, "No right, no wrong, or rules for me, I'm free," in the hit single "Let It Go."[3]

This kind of love cropped up in every movie, love song, and after-school television special I watched growing up, from *The Dead Poet's Society* to Sting's, "If You Love Someone, Set Them Free." The LGBT revolution of the early 2000s never would have occurred if the world had not already redefined love as giving people the chance to define and express themselves free of all moral constraint. "Heart plus heart equals marriage," says the bumper sticker.

I mention these pop cultural moments not just because this is how the culture "out there" defines love. Far too often, Christians also succumb to this understanding of love. The tragedy is, we should know better than to place ourselves at the center of the universe, as if the Bible taught, "For from us and through us and to us are all things. To us be praise and glory forever and ever, amen."

Note, however, that this man-centered love does correct, does make judgments, and does impose its own truths. All corrections, judgments, and truths, however, serve the purpose of giving people whatever they want. Such love even excommunicates. *If you don't let me be who I think I am and love whom I want to love, you are bigoted, intolerant, and hateful. I can have no communion with you.*

What Is Love?

Yet if we exchange this universe for a universe in which God is at the center of all things, yes, church discipline is loving. Church discipline at its core is about love. The Lord disciplines those he loves (Heb. 12:6). The same is true for us.

What is love in the Bible? It's easy to say what love is *like*. It's patient, kind, "does not envy or boast," is not rude or proud (1 Cor. 13:4–5).

It's also easy to say what love *does*. "It does not insist on its own way" (1 Cor. 13:5). It doesn't delight in evil but rejoices in the truth (v. 6). It works through truth (2 John 1–3). It "bears all things, believes all things, hopes all things, endures all things" (1 Cor. 13:7). It lays down its life for its friends (John 15:13).

Love also walks in Christ's commandments (2 John 6). Jesus says of himself, "I do as the Father has commanded me, so that the world may know that I love the Father" (John 14:31). And he says the same about us: "Whoever has my commandments and keeps them, he it is who loves me" (John 14:21). He even tells us that if we keep his commandments, we will abide in his love (John 15:10). And John says that if we keep God's word, God's love will be perfected in us (1 John 2:5).

Most of us need a radical reorientation of our understanding of love. In the Bible, love leads to obedience, and obedience is a sign of love.

Still, what exactly is love according to the Bible? How should we define it? I would say that *love is desiring another person's good, which is always God.*

Remember, "God is love" (1 John 4:8, 16). Which means all love is from God. Anything the world calls "love" that's not from God is not love. Because God is love.

We love people most, then, by pointing them to God, who is love. When people who claim to love God walk away from God, we love them most by correcting them and saying, "No, no, no. God is love. So if you want love, you must return to God." Those who oppose and disobey God are running away from love. They are choosing something besides love, even if they call it love.

If we want to pursue love, we must pursue God. We must follow after God, imitate God, walk in God's ways, listen to him, and do all that he says. Remember, he is love. Sure enough, Jesus models this love. He tells us that he abided in the Father's love by perfectly obeying the Father's commandments (John 15:10).

Love, the Bible teaches, is holy. You cannot have love apart from holiness. And true holiness always issues forth in love.

The relationship between love and holiness should help us understand the Bible's long-running theme of exclusion and exile. Passages like Matthew 18 and 1 Corinthians 5 don't offer us pictures of God doing something new or different. They present us a quick glimpse of what God always has done and will do. He has always removed sin from his presence, and he has always been working to remake a people in his own loving and righteous image. God excluded Adam and Eve from the garden. He excluded the fallen world from Noah's ark. He excluded the Canaanites from the promised land, and eventually he excluded his own people from the promised land. All the laws for the tabernacle also worked to exclude things that were unclean and unholy. And on the last day, God promises to exclude all whose faith doesn't rest in the finished work of Christ's incarnate life, substitutionary death, and death-defeating resurrection.

If you don't think excommunication is loving, you won't like the God of the Bible. God alone is at the center of the universe, and he alone is love. Therefore, in love, he excludes from himself everyone and everything that denies him because these are the deniers of love.

If God is love, we love people by sharing the gospel with them so that they might know God.

If God is love, we love people by teaching them everything God commands so that they might image God.

If God is love, we love people by correcting them when they walk away from God.

If God is love, we even love people by removing them from membership in the church when they insist on their own desires more than God because the only hope they have of life and love is to recognize that they are cutting themselves off from God. Therefore, we are trying to offer them the faintest whiff of what it means to be cut off now.

Fundamentally, then, churches should practice church discipline for love's sake: love for the sinner's sake, love for the other church members' sake, love for the non-Christian neighbor's sake, love for Christ's sake.

Clearing Up Some Lingering Questions

So, yes, church discipline is loving. But remember what I said earlier it must also be wise. For that reason, it's worth spending a little bit more time on some practical questions you may have.[4]

Which Sins Lead to Public Discipline?

One of the first questions people often ask about church discipline is which sins should a church formally and publicly discipline? After all, you might confront any sin quietly and privately. For instance, my wife might feel the need to gently admonish me—and this is *purely* hypothetical— for selfishly eating all the ice cream.

But even if she's right, and I am selfishly eating all the ice cream, and I continue in this pattern unrepentantly for years, this kind of sin probably shouldn't rise to the level of "telling it to the church."

So which sins warrant whole church involvement?

I believe the Bible teaches that formal, public church discipline is required in cases of *outward*, *significant*, and *unrepentant* sin—and it must be all three of those things.

A sin must have an *outward* manifestation. It must be something that can be seen with the eyes or heard with the ears. Again, think of Jesus's words about the necessity of two or three witnesses. Churches should not quickly throw the red flag of ejection every time they suspect greed or pride in someone's heart.

Second, a sin must be *significant*. A husband's selfishness of not leaving ice cream for his wife really is sin, but it's probably not the kind of sin that leaves a church wondering whether or not they can really affirm that man is a Christian. That's the criteria of significance, and yes, it's a subjective judgment. Is this the sort of sin that we assume Holy-Spirit indwelled Christians

36

should be *unable* to continue in indefinitely, at least when confronted? Does it leave us feeling like we can no longer affirm a profession of faith in Christ with integrity?

Finally, formal church discipline is the appropriate course of action when sin is *unrepentant*. The person involved in serious sin has been privately confronted with God's commands in Scripture, but he or she refuses to let go of the sin. From all appearances, the person prizes the sin more than Jesus.

How Long Should the Church Discipline Process Take?

Typically, determining whether a situation involves these three criteria takes a lot of time. How much time? It depends. The final step of excommunication should only occur once a church and its leaders feel confident that the person is unrepentant.

As a result, usually the process moves quite slowly, particularly when a sinner shows at least some interest in fighting against the sin. Listen to Paul: "admonish the idle, encourage the faint-hearted, help the weak, be patient with them all" (1 Thess. 5:14).

Sometimes, however, the process needs to speed up. This generally occurs when people are obviously determined to remain in their sin or when deceit is involved and words cannot be trusted. Situations of this sort can lead to immediate removal, like Paul describes in 1 Corinthians 5.

When Should Restoration Occur?

Restoration to the fellowship of the church occurs when there are signs of true repentance. What true repentance looks like depends on the nature of the sin. Sometimes repentance is a black and white matter, as with a man who has abandoned his wife. For him, repenting means returning to her, plain and simple. Yet sometimes repentance doesn't mean conquering a sin completely so much as demonstrating a new diligence in waging war against the sin, as with a person caught in a cycle of addiction.

Clearly, the question of true repentance is a difficult one that requires much wisdom. We must always balance caution with compassion. Some time may need to pass for repentance to be demonstrated by its fruits but not too much time (see 2 Cor. 2:5–8). Once a church decides to restore a repenting individual to its fellowship, there should be no talk of a probation period or second-class citizenship. Rather, the church should publicly pronounce its forgiveness (John 20:23), affirm its love for the repenting individual (2 Cor. 2:8), and celebrate (Luke 15:24).

By God's grace, I've witnessed a number of cases of church discipline where a person was removed from membership in the church and then restored months or even years later. Perhaps the story that stands out most in my memory involved a church member lying to and stealing money from church members to support a drug addiction. When caught, he refused to own up to his sin, and so the church removed him. Shortly thereafter he became homeless. Several years later, a young man in the church began reading the Bible with him. Little by little, this man's heart softened, and he began to repent. Then, on one glorious Sunday evening, he stood in front of the church and *preached* a several-page apology. He asked for God's forgiveness and ours. The church immediately restored him and cheered. God was glorified.

How Does a Church Practice Discipline?

Public accountability should be an outgrowth of what's already going on in the private lives of church members. Formal church discipline works best when members already know how to give and receive loving correction. They do it in their homes. They do it over lunch. They do it gently, carefully, and always with the good of the other person in mind. They don't offer corrective words selfishly—just to "get something off their chest."

Several other principles for conducting church discipline are crucial.

The process should involve as few people as possible. This principle clearly emerges from Matthew 18:15–17. If a one-on-one encounter yields repentance, good. If it takes two or three more, then leave it at that. A matter should only be taken to the whole church when all other avenues have been exhausted.

Individuals should receive the benefit of the doubt. As we have already observed, Jesus prescribes something like a careful judicial process in Matthew 18:16 "that every charge may be established by the evidence of two or three witnesses." Charges must be established. Evidence must be presented. Witnesses must be involved. Christians should move slowly and carefully, and churches should approach discipline cases with something like the courtroom principle of "innocent until proven guilty."

This principle applies not only in matters of formal discipline, it also affects how a Christian should confront a brother or sister in private. People must be given the benefit of the doubt. Questions should precede accusations. Clarity should be sought before certainties are pronounced. In the domain of discipline, as in every domain of life, "let every person be quick to hear, slow to speak, slow to anger" (James 1:19).

Church leaders should lead the process. Sin is deceitful and complex. It's easy to be deceived. Jude therefore writes, "have mercy on those who doubt; save others by snatching them out of the fire; to others show mercy with fear, hating even the garment stained by the flesh" (Jude 22–23). Generally speaking, once a matter of discipline moves beyond the first step or two, church elders should lead the process. The Holy Spirit has given them oversight over the whole congregation (Acts 20:28). Therefore, they should ordinarily be the ones determining whether a matter should go to the whole congregation.

Church discipline should involve the whole church. Different denominational traditions have different ways of involving the entire congregation in the process of formal discipline. But no matter the denomination, leaders should look for ways to "tell it to the church" (Matt. 18:17). Discipline, particularly in its final stages, is a deeply significant event in the life of a body, which, by virtue of our shared union in Christ, every part surely *does* own. Pastorally, it's a significant event that every part surely *should* own.

All will learn. All will be warned and challenged. All may have something to contribute.

Church Discipline Is Tough but Loving

In the final analysis, church discipline is tough but loving.

One time, my wife and I had to confront a close friend of ours over a terrible decision she was making in the workplace. She rejected our correction. We involved two more friends, and then two more. Each time she rebuffed our love. At several points through this process, which lasted a few weeks, I found myself with an upset stomach or having trouble sleeping on a couple of evenings—and neither of these things are normal for me. Yet we pressed ahead because we trusted that God is more loving and wiser than we are, and we could trust his word. Wonderfully, this woman eventually came back to us and told us that she had renounced the terrible work decision. Praise God. It was tough, but worth it.

Why should churches practice discipline? We do it for the sake of our evangelism and witness. If the church looks just like the world, why would anyone want to join it? If the young men are philanderers and the old men rich and stingy, if the young women are flirts and the old women alcoholics, how attractive will that church's witness be? How successful will their evangelism be?

Peter tells us to live such good lives in the world that, though people accuse you of doing wrong, "they may see [our] good deeds and glorify God" (1 Pet. 2:12). We should be distinct in our holiness, and we should be distinct in our love.

Again, why should churches practice discipline? In order to love like Jesus. Listen to him: "A new commandment I give to you, that you love one another: just as I have loved you, you also are to love one another. By this all people will know that you are my disciples, if you have love for one another" (John 13:34–35).

How did Jesus love us? By pursuing us in our sin, by laying down his life for our forgiveness, and by calling us to follow after him.

How then should we love each other? In the same way. We pursue each other in our sin, point to his sacrifice for forgiveness, and then help each other follow after him.

What will be the result? People will know that we are his disciples. Witness and love, correction and pursuit, are all bound up together.

Let me make this very personal: Who in your church are you open with about your sin? Who do you invite into your life to help you fight? And who do you help fight? Are you personally willing to speak the tough word to that brother or sister? If not, are you sure you love that brother or sister?

For Pastors:
Before You Practice
Church Discipline . . .

Pastors should not immediately begin practicing church discipline. They need to shepherd their congregations toward it slowly and carefully. How? Here are 10 steps:

1) Teach the gospel of repentance and faith, a gospel which tells people that Jesus is Savior, yes, but also Lord.
2) Teach the doctrine of conversion: that being born again means Jesus really changes you. Your life really looks different.
3) Teach and practice church membership. You cannot put somebody "out" if they

don't understand there is an "in" to be removed from.

4) Teach about church discipline. Teach multiple times and in multiple ways. Make sure others are teaching about it, and that you're not the only one. Hand out books or articles on discipline to the leaders of your congregation.

5) Teach about discipline in your new members class.

6) Cultivate a culture of discipleship, where it's seen as normal to speak openly into one another's lives. Model such openness and willingness to receive correction in your own life.

7) Get your church documents in shape. People should know what they are expected to believe as members of your church. And they should be able to see in your church constitution how discipline works and who is responsible.

8) Make sure your other leaders agree with it and believe it's biblical.

9) Do your best to make sure your membership rolls reflect who you see in regular attendance.

10) If it's the first time you're practicing church discipline, make sure it's an obvious sin that all Christians agree is wrong.

Notes

1. These five points drawn from 1 Corinthians 5 are quoted from Jonathan Leeman, "Church Discipline and the Love of God," Capitol Hill Baptist Church website, January 1, 2012, https://www.capitolhillbaptist.org/sermon/church-discipline-and-the-love-of-god/. This article is handed out in Capitol Hill's membership class.

2. Some material in this "Teach and Correct" section is quoted from Jonathan Leeman, "A Church Discipline Primer," 9Marks website, March 1, 2010, https://www.9marks.org/article/church-discipline-primer/.

3. *Frozen*, directed by Chris Buck and Jennifer Lee (Burbank, CA: Walt Disney Animation Studios, 2013).

4. Some material from this "Clearing Up Some Lingering Questions" section is quoted from Leeman, "A Church Discipline Primer."

Recommended Resources

For Pastors

Jonathan Leeman. *Church Discipline: How the Church Protects the Name of Jesus.* Wheaton, IL: Crossway, 2012.

For Pastors and Members

Jonathan Leeman. *The Rule of Love: How the Local Church Should Reflect God's Love and Authority.* Wheaton, IL: Crossway, 2018.

Jonathan Leeman. *Understanding Church Discipline.* Nashville, TN: B&H, 2016.

Scripture Index

IX 9Marks

Building Healthy Churches

9Marks exists to equip church leaders with a biblical vision and practical resources for displaying God's glory to the nations through healthy churches.

To that end, we want to see churches characterized by these nine marks of health:

1. Expositional Preaching
2. Biblical Theology
3. A Biblical Understanding of the Gospel
4. A Biblical Understanding of Conversion
5. A Biblical Understanding of Evangelism
6. Biblical Church Membership
7. Biblical Church Discipline
8. Biblical Discipleship
9. Biblical Church Leadership

Find all our Crossway titles and other resources at 9Marks.org.